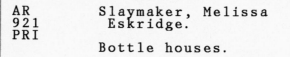

DATE			

Bottle Houses

The Creative World of Grandma Prisbrey

Melissa Eskridge Slaymaker

Illustrated by Julie Paschkis

Henry Holt and Company
New York

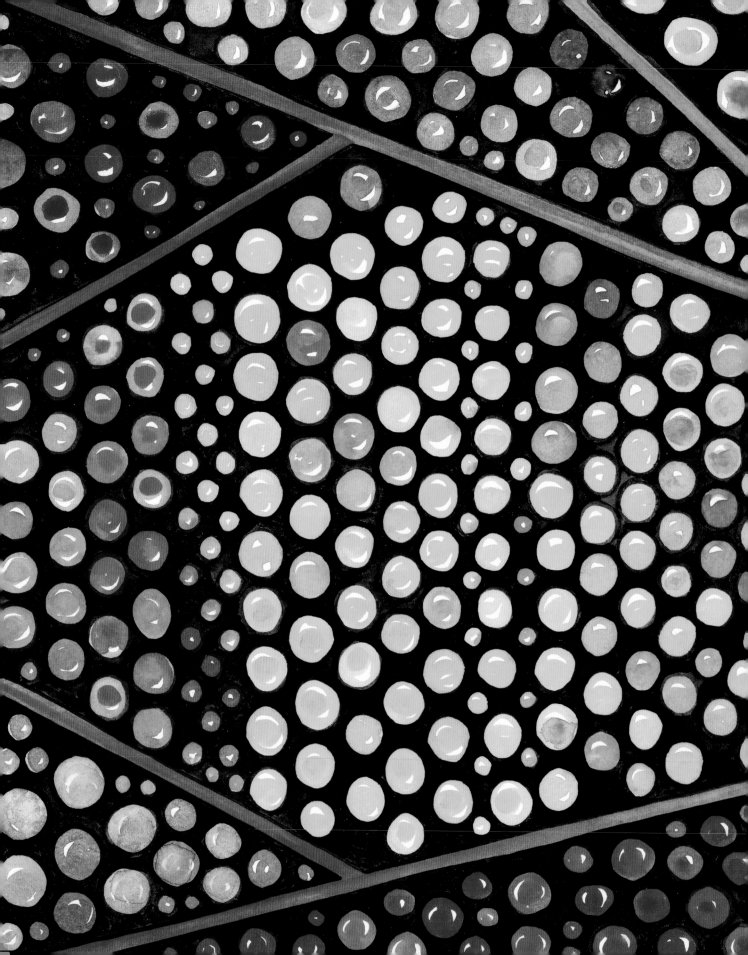

Being inside one of

Grandma Prisbrey's houses was like being inside

a rainbow or a kaleidoscope or a jewel. The walls

sparkled in sunlight, and in lamplight they glowed.

Some rooms were the colors of flame, others were shades

of sky; some were red as rubies, others were diamond-clear.

All shone like glass because glass is what they were.

Grandma Prisbrey lived in a bottle village.

For a long time Grandma Prisbey didn't live anywhere in particular, and she didn't have a house. She was too busy to have one. She'd been traveling around in a trailer with her family. She liked to keep reminders of where she'd been, but there's not much room for reminders in a travel trailer. So she collected pencils.

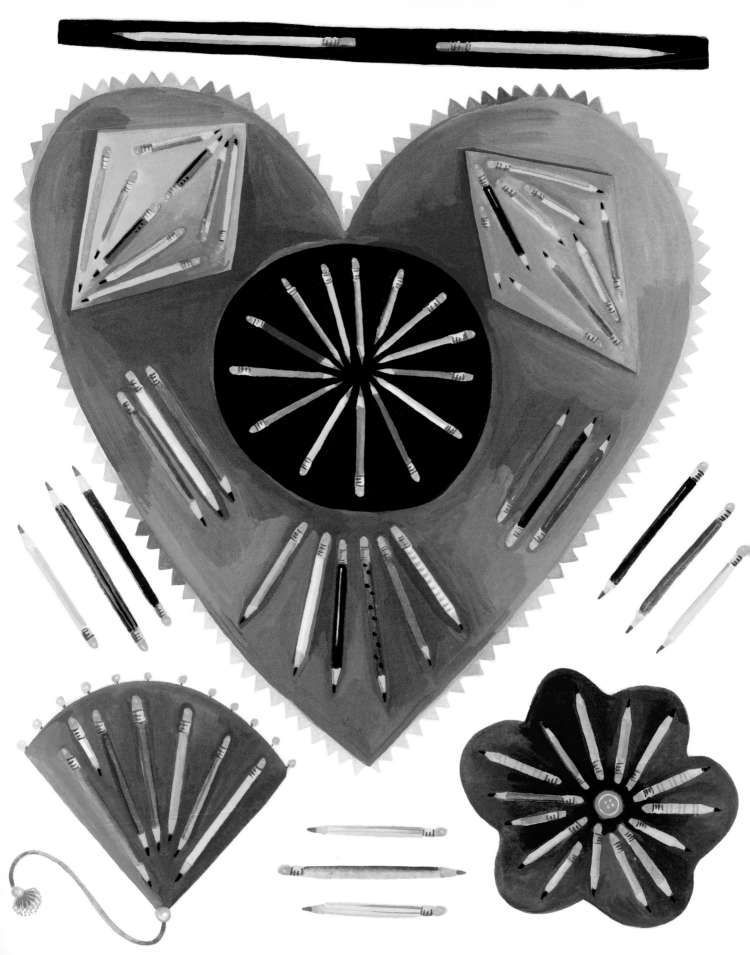

She had pencils from places
she'd been and people she'd met. There
were thousands of pencils—so many that
she started making things with them. She made
pencil flowers and fans, pencil people and patterns.
The pencils became more interesting that way,
and she wanted more room to display them.
She also wanted more room to settle down
when she wasn't traveling.

Grandma Prisbrey had some land in California, but she didn't have enough money to build a house in a regular way. But Grandma Prisbrey wasn't a regular sort of person who did things in a regular sort of way.

One day when she was visiting her land in California, she decided to drive down the road to the garbage dump to see if she could find something to build a house with.

"Everything under the sun shows up at the dump if you wait long enough," she said. "I found a photograph of the queen of England, a statue of a saint, and a crystal chandelier. What some people throw away, I believe I could wear to church."

At the dump, Grandma Prisbrey found bottles of every size and shape and color. There were clear bottles too, of course, but she liked the colorful ones best. Every day Grandma Prisbrey drove her truck to the dump and hauled stuff home.

"Lady," said the man who worked at the dump, "this place is going to make you famous someday."

Before long, there wasn't a bottle made that Grandma Prisbrey didn't have. And she had enough of them to build a house.

"A dairy inspector told me it's against the law to use milk bottles for anything but milk, so I quit using those," she said. "I've got plenty without them. The smallest bottle is a lady's ring. The biggest is a three-gallon whiskey bottle, made just for decoration, I hope!"

She stacked bottles to make walls, and all she had to buy was cement to hold them together.

She found everything else at the dump: furniture, stoves, refrigerators, dishes, clothes, batteries, lights, car parts, even dolls. Hundreds of dolls.

She built a bottle house for her pencil collection and
another one for her dolls.

She built a bottle chapel and a bottle birdbath.

She made a wishing well of blue bottles and a rumpus
room of green ones.

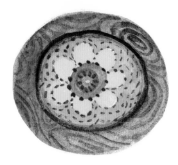

Just for fun she built
a round house. Everything in it
was round. It had a round fireplace,
a round bed, and a round dresser
with a round mirror
over it.

"I do all the work myself," she said. "Except for putting on roofs and doors. My sons do that."

And when she wanted a change from building with bottles, she tried other things.

For one of her sons she built a house of shells—shells of all kinds—and countless polished rocks and rhinestones. Nearby she made a singing tree. It had more than a thousand bottles hanging from it, and when the wind blew, the air resounded with the songs of tinkling glass chimes.

Grandma Prisbrey decided a pyramid might look nice, so she
built one of car headlights stacked five feet high, decorated with 150
gold lipstick cases and dozens of potted cactus.

"The cactus reminds me of myself," she said. "It's independent,
prickly, and asks nothing from anybody. And it blooms in all colors."

She liked all things to be colorful, including cats. Her cat had one green eye and one yellow. There were three fluffy kittens too, which Grandma Prisbrey dyed pink, green, and blue.

"I use vegetable dye so it doesn't hurt them," she explained. "My grandchildren love it."

Of course folks began to wonder
what was going on, and they started dropping by.
Just a few came at first, then a lot. Grandma Prisbrey
built a bottle cabana in the shade, where she served her
guests homemade cookies and lemonade.

With so many people walking around, sidewalks
seemed like a good idea. Grandma Prisbrey paved pretty
paths from place to place using odds and ends of this and
that—broken dishes and chipped tile, lost buttons and
bottle caps, shells and rocks.

By the time she was done, Grandma Prisbrey
had a bottle village with fountains and a cactus garden.
Visitors came from all over to see it.

"They call me an artist," she said, "even though I can't draw a car that looks like one. But I guess there are different kinds of art."

The mosaic sidewalk and the wall that surrounds Bottle Village

The headlight pyramid stands in front of the round house

A display from Grandma Prisbrey's pencil collection

Sunlight makes the colored bottles glow inside the round house

The wishing well and some of Grandma's cactus

Tressa "Grandma" Prisbrey was born in 1896, began building her bottle village in 1956, and died in 1988. By 1966 most of the construction was complete, including twenty-two sculptures and thirteen one-room buildings she called houses. In 1996 Grandma Prisbrey's Bottle Village was listed in the National Register of Historic Places. It is a City of Simi Valley and County of Ventura Cultural Landmark, and a State of California Historical Landmark. Bottle Village suffered extensive damage in the 1994 earthquake, and the Preserve Bottle Village Committee is currently working to raise funds for its restoration. You can visit their Web site at:

http://echomatic.home.mindspring.com/bv

For Emma, my colorful and visionary child,
and for Chris, who showed me the value of things that last —M. E. S.

For Gwen —J. P.

Many thanks to the Preserve Bottle Village Committee for their invaluable help,
and to Rebecca Hoffberger, founder and director of the American Visionary Art Museum in Baltimore

Henry Holt and Company, LLC
Publishers since 1866
115 West 18th Street, New York, New York 10011
www.henryholt.com

Henry Holt is a registered trademark of Henry Holt and Company, LLC
Text copyright © 2004 by Melissa Eskridge Slaymaker. Illustrations copyright © 2004 by Julie Paschkis.
All rights reserved. Distributed in Canada by H. B. Fenn and Company Ltd.

Library of Congress Cataloging-in-Publication Data
Slaymaker, Melissa Eskridge.
Bottle houses: the creative world of Grandma Prisbrey / Melissa Eskridge Slaymaker; illustrated by Julie Paschkis.
p.   cm.
Summary: An introduction to the world of folk artist Grandma Prisbrey.
1. Prisbrey, Tressa—Juvenile literature. 2. Folk artists—California—Biography—Juvenile literature. 3. Refuse as art material—
California—Juvenile literature. 4. Vernacular architecture—California—Juvenile literature. [1. Prisbrey, Tressa. 2. Artists.
3. Women—Biography.] I. Paschkis, Julie, ill. II. Title.   NK512.P75S58 2004   745'.092—dc21   2003007064
ISBN 0-8050-7131-8 / First Edition—2004
Printed in the United States of America on acid-free paper. ∞

1 3 5 7 9 10 8 6 4 2

The artist used Winsor & Newton gouaches on Arches paper to create the illustrations for this book.
Photo credits: page 30 (upper left, upper right, lower left) © Bilyana Dimitrova (www.bdphotography.com); page 30 (lower right)
Melissa Eskridge Slaymaker; page 31 (top—portrait of Grandma Prisbrey) Amanda Devine; page 31 (bottom) Julie Paschkis.
All quotes attributed to Grandma Prisbrey were taken from *Grandma's Bottle Village* by Grandma Prisbrey
and used with the permission of the Preserve Bottle Village Committee.

A portion of the proceeds from this book will go to:
Preserve Bottle Village Committee
P.O. Box 1412, Simi Valley, California, 93062
http://echomatic.home.mindspring.com/bv